EMMANUEL JOSEPH

The Mindful Marketplace, Bridging Politics, Psychology, and Health in Modern Business

Copyright © 2025 by Emmanuel Joseph

All rights reserved. No part of this publication may be reproduced, stored or transmitted in any form or by any means, electronic, mechanical, photocopying, recording, scanning, or otherwise without written permission from the publisher. It is illegal to copy this book, post it to a website, or distribute it by any other means without permission.

First edition

This book was professionally typeset on Reedsy.
Find out more at reedsy.com

Contents

1	Chapter 1: Introduction to the Mindful Marketplace	1
2	Chapter 2: The Political Landscape and Business	3
3	Chapter 3: The Psychology of Consumer Behavior	5
4	Chapter 4: Employee Well-being and Organizational Health	7
5	Chapter 5: The Intersection of Business and Health	9
6	Chapter 6: Emotional Intelligence in Leadership	11
7	Chapter 7: The Role of Ethics in Business	13
8	Chapter 8: Sustainability in the Mindful Marketplace	15
9	Chapter 9: The Power of Corporate Social Responsibility	17
10	Chapter 10: The Role of Technology in Modern Business	19
11	Chapter 11: Navigating Economic Challenges	21
12	Chapter 12: Building a Positive Organizational Culture	23
13	Chapter 13: The Future of the Mindful Marketplace	25
14	Chapter 14: Mindfulness and Decision-Making in Business	27
15	Chapter 15: Integrating Psychology into Business Strategy	29
16	Chapter 16: The Role of Innovation in Business Success	31
17	Chapter 17: Conclusion and Future Directions	33

1

Chapter 1: Introduction to the Mindful Marketplace

In today's fast-paced and interconnected world, businesses are no longer isolated entities focused solely on profit. They are part of a larger ecosystem where politics, psychology, and health play crucial roles in shaping their success. This book explores how modern businesses can thrive by embracing mindfulness and integrating these three critical domains. It delves into the intricacies of the marketplace, highlighting the importance of understanding political dynamics, psychological insights, and health considerations in decision-making processes.

The concept of the mindful marketplace goes beyond traditional business strategies. It emphasizes the need for businesses to be aware of their impact on society and the environment. By fostering a culture of mindfulness, companies can make more informed decisions that benefit not only their bottom line but also the well-being of their employees, customers, and the community at large. This chapter sets the stage for a comprehensive exploration of how mindfulness can bridge the gap between politics, psychology, and health in the business world.

Political factors have always influenced the business landscape, but their significance has grown exponentially in recent years. From regulatory changes to geopolitical tensions, businesses must navigate a complex web of political dynamics. This chapter examines how political awareness can help businesses anticipate and adapt to changes in the political environment, thereby reducing risks and seizing opportunities. By understanding the interplay between politics and business, companies can develop strategies that align with broader societal goals.

Psychology, on the other hand, provides valuable insights into human behavior, motivation, and decision-making. In the context of the mindful marketplace, understanding psychological principles can help businesses create more effective marketing campaigns, improve customer experiences, and enhance employee engagement. This chapter explores the psychological underpinnings of consumer behavior and highlights the importance of empathy, emotional intelligence, and ethical considerations in business practices. By tapping into the power of psychology, businesses can build stronger relationships with their stakeholders and foster a positive organizational culture.

2

Chapter 2: The Political Landscape and Business

The business environment is deeply intertwined with the political landscape. Political decisions, policies, and regulations can significantly impact the way businesses operate. This chapter delves into the various ways in which politics influences business and how companies can navigate this complex terrain. From understanding the implications of government policies to engaging in corporate lobbying, businesses must develop strategies to effectively manage political risks and capitalize on opportunities.

Government policies and regulations play a crucial role in shaping the business environment. Taxation, labor laws, environmental regulations, and trade policies are just a few examples of how political decisions can affect businesses. Companies need to stay informed about these policies and anticipate changes that could impact their operations. This chapter explores how businesses can engage with policymakers, participate in public consultations, and advocate for favorable policies that align with their goals and values.

Corporate lobbying is another important aspect of the political-business nexus. Through lobbying efforts, businesses can influence legislation and regulations that affect their industry. While lobbying is often viewed with suspicion, it can be a legitimate way for businesses to protect their interests and contribute to policymaking. This chapter examines the ethical considerations and best practices for corporate lobbying, highlighting the importance of transparency, accountability, and integrity in these efforts.

In addition to domestic politics, businesses must also consider the global political landscape. Geopolitical tensions, international trade agreements, and foreign policies can have far-reaching implications for companies operating in multiple countries. This chapter explores how businesses can navigate the complexities of international politics, build strategic alliances, and mitigate risks associated with geopolitical instability. By adopting a proactive and informed approach to political engagement, businesses can enhance their resilience and thrive in a rapidly changing world.

3

Chapter 3: The Psychology of Consumer Behavior

Understanding consumer behavior is essential for businesses aiming to succeed in the marketplace. Psychology provides valuable insights into the factors that influence consumer decisions, from cognitive biases to emotional responses. This chapter explores the psychological underpinnings of consumer behavior and how businesses can leverage these insights to create more effective marketing strategies, improve customer experiences, and drive sales.

Cognitive biases are systematic patterns of deviation from rationality in judgment and decision-making. These biases can significantly impact consumer behavior, leading to predictable errors in judgment. This chapter examines some of the most common cognitive biases, such as the availability heuristic, confirmation bias, and the anchoring effect. By understanding these biases, businesses can design marketing campaigns that resonate with consumers, influence their choices, and drive engagement.

Emotions play a crucial role in shaping consumer behavior. Emotional responses can influence purchase decisions, brand loyalty, and customer satisfaction. This chapter delves into the various ways in which emotions impact consumer behavior, from the role of positive emotions in driving impulse purchases to the impact of negative emotions on brand perception.

Businesses can harness the power of emotions to create memorable experiences, build emotional connections with customers, and foster brand loyalty.

In addition to cognitive biases and emotions, social influences also play a significant role in consumer behavior. Social norms, peer pressure, and cultural factors can shape consumer choices and preferences. This chapter explores the social aspects of consumer behavior and how businesses can leverage social influence to enhance their marketing efforts. By understanding the social dynamics that drive consumer behavior, businesses can create strategies that tap into the power of social proof, word-of-mouth marketing, and influencer endorsements.

4

Chapter 4: Employee Well-being and Organizational Health

The success of a business is closely linked to the well-being of its employees. A healthy and engaged workforce is more productive, innovative, and resilient. This chapter explores the importance of employee well-being and organizational health, highlighting the key factors that contribute to a positive work environment and how businesses can foster a culture of well-being.

Employee well-being encompasses physical, mental, and emotional health. Businesses need to adopt a holistic approach to employee well-being, addressing not only physical health but also mental and emotional well-being. This chapter examines the various factors that influence employee well-being, such as work-life balance, stress management, and access to health resources. By prioritizing employee well-being, businesses can create a supportive and nurturing work environment that enhances overall performance and job satisfaction.

Organizational health goes beyond individual well-being to encompass the overall functioning and effectiveness of the organization. It involves factors such as leadership, communication, and organizational culture. This chapter explores the key elements of organizational health and how businesses can cultivate a positive organizational culture that promotes collaboration, innovation, and resilience. By fostering a healthy organizational environment, businesses can enhance employee engagement, reduce turnover, and drive long-term success.

Leadership plays a crucial role in shaping employee well-being and organizational health. Effective leaders inspire, motivate, and support their teams, creating a positive and inclusive work environment. This chapter examines the qualities of effective leaders and how they can promote employee well-being and organizational health. By adopting a mindful and empathetic approach to leadership, businesses can create a culture of trust, respect, and collaboration that enhances overall performance and well-being.

In addition to leadership, communication is a key factor in promoting employee well-being and organizational health. Open and transparent communication fosters trust, reduces uncertainty, and enhances employee engagement. This chapter explores the importance of effective communication and how businesses can implement strategies to improve communication within the organization. By fostering a culture of open communication, businesses can create a more connected and engaged workforce that drives success.

5

Chapter 5: The Intersection of Business and Health

Health is a crucial consideration for modern businesses. The well-being of employees, customers, and the community at large can significantly impact a company's success. This chapter explores the intersection of business and health, highlighting the importance of health initiatives, workplace wellness programs, and corporate social responsibility in promoting a healthier society.

Workplace wellness programs have gained popularity in recent years as businesses recognize the benefits of investing in employee health. These programs can include a range of initiatives, such as fitness challenges, mental health support, and healthy eating campaigns. By promoting a culture of health and wellness, businesses can improve employee morale, reduce absenteeism, and enhance overall productivity. This chapter examines the key components of effective workplace wellness programs and how businesses can implement them to support employee well-being.

Corporate social responsibility (CSR) is another important aspect of the intersection between business and health. Companies have a responsibility to contribute to the well-being of the communities they serve. This chapter explores how businesses can engage in CSR initiatives that promote health and wellness, such as supporting local health clinics, funding public health campaigns, and advocating for policies that improve public health. By prioritizing health in their CSR efforts, businesses can make a positive impact on society and build stronger relationships with their stakeholders.

In addition to employee and community health, businesses must also consider the health and safety of their customers. Product safety, transparency, and ethical marketing practices are essential for building trust and maintaining a positive reputation. This chapter examines the importance of consumer health and how businesses can ensure the safety and well-being of their customers. By adopting ethical practices and prioritizing consumer health, businesses can build brand loyalty and drive long-term success.

The COVID-19 pandemic has underscored the importance of health in the business world. Companies have had to adapt to new health protocols, remote work arrangements, and changing consumer behaviors. This chapter explores the lessons learned from the pandemic and how businesses can build resilience in the face of future health crises. By embracing a proactive approach to health, businesses can navigate uncertainties and continue to thrive in a rapidly changing world.

6

Chapter 6: Emotional Intelligence in Leadership

Effective leadership is essential for the success of any business. In the context of the mindful marketplace, emotional intelligence (EI) is a critical skill for leaders. This chapter explores the importance of emotional intelligence in leadership and how it can enhance decision-making, communication, and relationship-building within the organization.

Emotional intelligence involves the ability to recognize, understand, and manage one's own emotions, as well as the emotions of others. Leaders with high emotional intelligence are better equipped to handle stress, navigate conflicts, and build strong relationships with their teams. This chapter examines the key components of emotional intelligence, such as self-awareness, self-regulation, empathy, and social skills. By developing these skills, leaders can create a more positive and inclusive work environment.

Self-awareness is the foundation of emotional intelligence. Leaders who are self-aware are better able to understand their strengths and weaknesses, recognize their emotional triggers, and make more informed decisions. This chapter explores the importance of self-awareness in leadership and how leaders can cultivate this skill through reflection, feedback, and mindfulness practices. By becoming more self-aware, leaders can enhance their emotional intelligence and improve their overall effectiveness.

Empathy is another critical component of emotional intelligence. Leaders who are empathetic can understand and respond to the emotions and needs of their team members. This chapter examines the role of empathy in leadership and how it can foster a culture of trust, collaboration, and support. By practicing empathy, leaders can build stronger relationships with their teams, enhance communication, and create a more inclusive and positive work environment.

Social skills are essential for effective leadership. Leaders with strong social skills can build and maintain relationships, influence others, and navigate social dynamics within the organization. This chapter explores the importance of social skills in leadership and how leaders can develop these skills through active listening, effective communication, and conflict resolution. By enhancing their social skills, leaders can create a more cohesive and motivated team that drives organizational success.

7

Chapter 7: The Role of Ethics in Business

Ethics play a crucial role in the success and sustainability of businesses. In the mindful marketplace, ethical considerations are at the forefront of decision-making processes. This chapter explores the importance of ethics in business and how companies can uphold ethical standards in their operations, interactions, and strategies.

Ethical business practices involve adhering to moral principles and values, such as honesty, integrity, fairness, and respect. This chapter examines the key elements of ethical business practices and how they can guide decision-making and behavior within the organization. By prioritizing ethics, businesses can build trust with their stakeholders, enhance their reputation, and create a positive impact on society.

Transparency is a fundamental aspect of ethical business practices. Companies that are transparent about their operations, policies, and performance can build trust with their stakeholders and foster a culture of accountability. This chapter explores the importance of transparency in business and how companies can implement transparent practices, such as open communication, clear reporting, and ethical marketing. By being transparent, businesses can build stronger relationships with their customers, employees, and investors.

Corporate governance is another important aspect of business ethics. Effective corporate governance involves establishing systems and processes that ensure accountability, transparency, and ethical behavior within the organization. This chapter examines the role of corporate governance in promoting ethical business practices and how companies can implement strong governance frameworks. By prioritizing corporate governance, businesses can enhance their credibility, reduce risks, and drive long-term success.

Ethical leadership is essential for fostering a culture of ethics within the organization. Leaders who model ethical behavior and promote ethical standards can influence the actions and decisions of their teams. This chapter explores the importance of ethical leadership and how leaders can uphold and promote ethical principles within the organization. By practicing ethical leadership, businesses can create a culture of integrity, trust, and respect that drives organizational success.

8

Chapter 8: Sustainability in the Mindful Marketplace

Sustainability has become a critical consideration for businesses in the modern marketplace. As environmental concerns continue to rise, companies are increasingly expected to adopt sustainable practices that minimize their impact on the planet. This chapter explores the importance of sustainability in business and how companies can integrate sustainable practices into their operations, products, and strategies.

Sustainable business practices involve adopting methods that reduce environmental impact, conserve resources, and promote social responsibility. This chapter examines the key elements of sustainable business practices, such as energy efficiency, waste reduction, and responsible sourcing. By prioritizing sustainability, businesses can not only reduce their environmental footprint but also enhance their reputation and appeal to environmentally conscious consumers.

One of the most effective ways for businesses to promote sustainability is through innovation. This chapter explores how businesses can leverage technological advancements and innovative solutions to address environmental challenges. From developing eco-friendly products to implementing sustainable supply chain practices, companies can drive positive change and contribute to a more sustainable future. By embracing innovation, businesses can stay ahead of regulatory requirements and meet the growing demand for sustainable products and services.

Corporate sustainability also involves engaging with stakeholders and fostering a culture of sustainability within the organization. This chapter examines how businesses can engage employees, customers, and partners in their sustainability efforts. By fostering a culture of sustainability, businesses can create a sense of shared responsibility and drive collective action towards a more sustainable future. This chapter also explores the importance of transparency and accountability in sustainability reporting, highlighting best practices for communicating sustainability initiatives and progress.

9

Chapter 9: The Power of Corporate Social Responsibility

Corporate social responsibility (CSR) is a key aspect of the mindful marketplace. Businesses are increasingly expected to act as responsible corporate citizens, contributing to the well-being of society and addressing social and environmental challenges. This chapter explores the importance of CSR and how businesses can effectively implement and communicate their CSR initiatives.

CSR involves a wide range of activities, from philanthropy and community engagement to environmental sustainability and ethical business practices. This chapter examines the different dimensions of CSR and how businesses can develop comprehensive CSR strategies that align with their values and goals. By adopting a strategic approach to CSR, businesses can create meaningful and lasting impact on society while enhancing their brand reputation and stakeholder relationships.

One of the key challenges in CSR is measuring and communicating impact. This chapter explores the importance of transparency and accountability in CSR reporting and how businesses can effectively measure and communicate their CSR efforts. By providing clear and accurate information about their CSR initiatives, businesses can build trust with their stakeholders and demonstrate their commitment to social and environmental responsibility.

Collaboration is another important aspect of effective CSR. This chapter examines how businesses can partner with other organizations, such as non-profits, government agencies, and community groups, to amplify their impact. By working together, businesses can leverage resources, expertise, and networks to address complex social and environmental challenges. This chapter also explores the role of employee engagement in CSR, highlighting best practices for involving employees in CSR initiatives and fostering a culture of social responsibility within the organization.

10

Chapter 10: The Role of Technology in Modern Business

Technology has revolutionized the business landscape, transforming the way companies operate, communicate, and interact with their stakeholders. This chapter explores the role of technology in modern business and how companies can leverage technological advancements to drive innovation, efficiency, and growth.

Digital transformation is a key aspect of the modern business environment. This chapter examines the importance of digital transformation and how businesses can harness the power of technology to streamline operations, enhance customer experiences, and improve decision-making. From adopting cloud computing and artificial intelligence to implementing data analytics and automation, businesses can leverage technology to stay competitive and drive growth.

Innovation is another critical aspect of the role of technology in business. This chapter explores how businesses can foster a culture of innovation and leverage technological advancements to develop new products, services, and business models. By embracing innovation, businesses can stay ahead of market trends, meet evolving customer needs, and drive long-term success. This chapter also examines the role of research and development (R&D) in driving innovation and how businesses can invest in R&D to stay at the forefront of technological advancements.

Technology also plays a crucial role in enhancing communication and collaboration within the organization. This chapter explores how businesses can leverage digital tools and platforms to improve communication, collaboration, and knowledge sharing. By adopting technologies such as video conferencing, project management software, and collaboration platforms, businesses can create a more connected and productive workforce.

The ethical considerations of technology are also important for modern businesses. This chapter examines the ethical implications of technological advancements and how businesses can navigate the ethical challenges associated with technology. From data privacy and security to the impact of automation on employment, businesses must consider the ethical implications of their technological decisions. By adopting ethical practices and prioritizing responsible technology use, businesses can build trust with their stakeholders and contribute to a more equitable and ethical business environment.

11

Chapter 11: Navigating Economic Challenges

Economic challenges are an inevitable part of the business landscape. From recessions and inflation to market fluctuations and global economic crises, businesses must be prepared to navigate these challenges effectively. This chapter explores the importance of economic resilience and how businesses can develop strategies to weather economic storms and emerge stronger.

Economic resilience involves the ability of a business to withstand and adapt to economic shocks and uncertainties. This chapter examines the key components of economic resilience, such as financial planning, diversification, and risk management. By adopting a proactive approach to economic challenges, businesses can minimize the impact of economic downturns and position themselves for long-term success. This chapter also explores the role of government policies and economic support measures in helping businesses navigate economic challenges.

One of the key strategies for navigating economic challenges is diversification. This chapter explores how businesses can diversify their products, services, and markets to reduce their reliance on a single revenue stream. By diversifying, businesses can spread their risks and create new opportunities for growth. This chapter also examines the importance of agility and flexibility in responding to economic changes. Businesses that can quickly adapt to changing market conditions are better positioned to thrive in uncertain economic environments.

Financial planning and risk management are essential for building economic resilience. This chapter explores the importance of sound financial management practices, such as budgeting, forecasting, and cash flow management. By maintaining healthy financial practices, businesses can build a strong financial foundation that allows them to withstand economic challenges. This chapter also examines the role of risk management in identifying, assessing, and mitigating potential economic risks. By implementing effective risk management strategies, businesses can protect themselves from economic shocks and uncertainties.

12

Chapter 12: Building a Positive Organizational Culture

A positive organizational culture is essential for the success and sustainability of a business. It influences employee behavior, motivation, and overall performance. This chapter explores the importance of building a positive organizational culture and how businesses can create a supportive and inclusive work environment that fosters collaboration, innovation, and engagement.

Organizational culture refers to the shared values, beliefs, and norms that shape the behavior of employees within the organization. This chapter examines the key elements of a positive organizational culture, such as trust, respect, and open communication. By fostering a positive culture, businesses can create a work environment where employees feel valued, supported, and motivated to contribute their best efforts. This chapter also explores the role of leadership in shaping and promoting a positive organizational culture.

Diversity and inclusion are critical components of a positive organizational culture. This chapter examines the importance of diversity and inclusion in creating a dynamic and innovative workforce. By embracing diversity, businesses can benefit from a wide range of perspectives, ideas, and experiences. This chapter explores best practices for promoting diversity and inclusion, such as implementing inclusive hiring practices, providing diversity training, and creating employee resource groups. By fostering an inclusive culture, businesses can create a more equitable and engaging work environment.

Employee engagement is another important aspect of a positive organizational culture. This chapter explores how businesses can enhance employee engagement through recognition, feedback, and professional development opportunities. Engaged employees are more likely to be productive, innovative, and committed to the success of the organization. This chapter also examines the importance of work-life balance in promoting employee well-being and engagement. By supporting work-life balance, businesses can create a healthier and more sustainable work environment.

13

Chapter 13: The Future of the Mindful Marketplace

The future of the mindful marketplace is shaped by emerging trends, technological advancements, and evolving societal expectations. This chapter explores the future of business and how companies can stay ahead of the curve by embracing innovation, sustainability, and social responsibility.

One of the key trends shaping the future of the mindful marketplace is the rise of conscious consumerism. Consumers are increasingly making purchasing decisions based on ethical, environmental, and social considerations. This chapter examines how businesses can respond to the growing demand for ethical and sustainable products and services. By aligning their values with those of conscious consumers, businesses can build brand loyalty and drive long-term success.

Technological advancements will continue to play a significant role in shaping the future of business. This chapter explores the potential of emerging technologies, such as artificial intelligence, blockchain, and the Internet of Things (IoT), to transform the business landscape. By staying abreast of technological trends and investing in innovation, businesses can harness the power of technology to drive efficiency, improve customer experiences, and create new opportunities for growth.

Sustainability will remain a critical consideration for businesses in the future. This chapter examines the importance of sustainable business practices and how companies can continue to innovate and evolve to meet environmental challenges. From adopting circular economy principles to investing in renewable energy, businesses can play a leading role in creating a more sustainable future. This chapter also explores the role of policy and regulation in promoting sustainability and how businesses can engage with policymakers to drive positive change.

The future of the mindful marketplace is also shaped by the evolving expectations of employees, customers, and stakeholders. This chapter explores how businesses can build stronger relationships with their stakeholders by prioritizing transparency, accountability, and social responsibility. By fostering a culture of trust and collaboration, businesses can navigate the complexities of the future and drive long-term success.

14

Chapter 14: Mindfulness and Decision-Making in Business

Mindfulness is a powerful tool that can enhance decision-making in business. It involves being fully present and aware of the moment, allowing individuals to make more informed and thoughtful decisions. This chapter explores the importance of mindfulness in business and how it can improve decision-making processes, reduce stress, and foster a more positive work environment.

Mindful decision-making involves being aware of one's thoughts, emotions, and biases, and considering the broader impact of decisions on various stakeholders. This chapter examines the key principles of mindful decision-making, such as staying present, practicing self-reflection, and considering long-term consequences. By adopting a mindful approach to decision-making, businesses can make more ethical and sustainable choices that benefit both the organization and society.

Mindfulness can also help reduce stress and improve focus, leading to better decision-making. This chapter explores the various mindfulness practices that can be integrated into the workplace, such as meditation, deep breathing exercises, and mindful communication. By promoting mindfulness in the workplace, businesses can create a more supportive and resilient work environment, where employees feel empowered to make thoughtful decisions.

The benefits of mindfulness extend beyond individual well-being to the overall success of the organization. This chapter examines how mindfulness can enhance organizational performance by fostering a culture of collaboration, innovation, and continuous improvement. By embracing mindfulness, businesses can create a more adaptive and agile organization that is better equipped to navigate the complexities of the modern marketplace.

Mindfulness is not just a personal practice, but a collective effort that requires the commitment and support of the entire organization. This chapter explores how businesses can cultivate a culture of mindfulness by providing training, resources, and support for employees. By integrating mindfulness into the fabric of the organization, businesses can create a more mindful and purposeful work environment that drives long-term success.

15

Chapter 15: Integrating Psychology into Business Strategy

Psychology offers valuable insights that can enhance business strategy. Understanding human behavior, motivation, and decision-making processes can help businesses create more effective marketing campaigns, improve customer experiences, and foster a positive organizational culture. This chapter explores how businesses can integrate psychological principles into their strategies to drive success.

One of the key ways businesses can leverage psychology is through understanding consumer behavior. This chapter examines how psychological principles, such as cognitive biases, social influence, and emotional responses, can impact consumer decisions. By incorporating these insights into their marketing strategies, businesses can create more persuasive and engaging campaigns that resonate with their target audience. This chapter also explores the importance of empathy and emotional intelligence in understanding and connecting with customers.

Employee motivation and engagement are critical for organizational success. This chapter explores how businesses can apply psychological principles to create a motivating and supportive work environment. By understanding the factors that drive employee motivation, such as intrinsic and extrinsic rewards, businesses can develop strategies to enhance job satisfaction and performance. This chapter also examines the role of positive reinforcement, goal-setting, and feedback in fostering a culture of high performance and continuous improvement.

Leadership is another area where psychology can play a significant role. This chapter explores how psychological insights can enhance leadership effectiveness. By understanding the psychological needs of their team members, leaders can adopt a more empathetic and supportive approach. This chapter also examines the importance of self-awareness, emotional intelligence, and effective communication in leadership. By integrating psychological principles into their leadership practices, businesses can create a more positive and cohesive organizational culture.

Organizational change is often met with resistance, but psychological insights can help businesses navigate change more effectively. This chapter explores how businesses can apply psychological principles to manage change and foster a culture of adaptability. By understanding the psychological factors that contribute to resistance, businesses can develop strategies to address concerns, build support, and facilitate a smoother transition. This chapter also examines the role of communication, training, and employee involvement in managing organizational change.

16

Chapter 16: The Role of Innovation in Business Success

Innovation is a driving force behind business success in the modern marketplace. It involves the creation and implementation of new ideas, products, services, and processes that can enhance a company's competitiveness and growth. This chapter explores the importance of innovation in business and how companies can foster a culture of innovation to drive long-term success.

Innovation begins with a mindset that values creativity, curiosity, and a willingness to take risks. This chapter examines the key principles of an innovative mindset and how businesses can cultivate this mindset within their teams. By encouraging employees to think outside the box, experiment, and learn from failures, businesses can create an environment where innovation thrives. This chapter also explores the role of leadership in fostering a culture of innovation, highlighting the importance of visionary leadership and support for creative endeavors.

Collaboration is a critical component of innovation. This chapter examines how businesses can foster collaboration both within and outside the organization to drive innovation. By breaking down silos and encouraging cross-functional teamwork, businesses can tap into a diverse range of perspectives and ideas. This chapter also explores the benefits of external collaboration, such as partnerships with startups, academic institutions, and industry consortia. By leveraging external networks and resources, businesses can accelerate innovation and stay ahead of market trends.

Investing in research and development (R&D) is essential for driving innovation. This chapter examines the importance of R&D and how businesses can allocate resources to support innovative projects. By investing in R&D, businesses can develop new technologies, products, and services that meet evolving customer needs and market demands. This chapter also explores the role of intellectual property (IP) in protecting and commercializing innovative ideas. By securing patents, trademarks, and copyrights, businesses can safeguard their innovations and gain a competitive edge.

Innovation is not limited to product development; it also involves process innovation. This chapter explores how businesses can improve their operational processes to enhance efficiency, reduce costs, and improve customer experiences. By adopting lean principles, automation, and data-driven decision-making, businesses can optimize their operations and create value for their stakeholders. This chapter also examines the role of digital transformation in driving process innovation, highlighting the importance of adopting new technologies and data analytics to streamline operations.

17

Chapter 17: Conclusion and Future Directions

As we draw to the end of this exploration of the mindful marketplace, it's clear that the integration of politics, psychology, and health in modern business is not just beneficial but essential. Businesses that embrace mindfulness and consider the broader impact of their decisions are better positioned to thrive in a complex and interconnected world. This final chapter synthesizes the key insights from the book and offers guidance on how businesses can continue to evolve and succeed in the future.

The mindful marketplace calls for businesses to be aware of their impact on society and the environment. By fostering a culture of mindfulness, businesses can make more informed decisions that benefit not only their bottom line but also the well-being of their employees, customers, and the community at large. This chapter revisits the importance of integrating political awareness, psychological insights, and health considerations into business practices. By doing so, businesses can create a more sustainable, ethical, and resilient future.

As we move forward, businesses must continue to embrace innovation and adaptability. The future is uncertain, and the ability to navigate change and seize opportunities will be crucial for long-term success. This chapter explores how businesses can stay ahead of emerging trends and technological advancements by fostering a culture of continuous learning and improvement. By investing in research and development, embracing digital transformation, and encouraging creativity, businesses can drive innovation and stay competitive in the ever-evolving marketplace.

The mindful marketplace also emphasizes the importance of collaboration and partnerships. Businesses cannot achieve their goals in isolation; they must work together with stakeholders, including employees, customers, government agencies, and non-profits, to drive positive change. This chapter examines the role of collaboration in achieving business success and how businesses can build strong relationships and alliances to address complex challenges. By fostering a spirit of cooperation and mutual support, businesses can create a more inclusive and resilient marketplace.

In conclusion, the mindful marketplace offers a holistic approach to business that considers the interconnectedness of politics, psychology, and health. By embracing mindfulness and integrating these critical domains into their strategies, businesses can create a positive and lasting impact on society. The future of business lies in the hands of those who are willing to be mindful, innovative, and collaborative. As we move forward, let us strive to build a marketplace that is not only profitable but also ethical, sustainable, and human-centered.

Description: "The Mindful Marketplace: Bridging Politics, Psychology, and Health in Modern Business"

In "The Mindful Marketplace: Bridging Politics, Psychology, and Health in Modern Business," we explore the dynamic interplay between politics, psychology, and health in today's business environment. This comprehensive guide delves into how these three critical domains shape the modern marketplace and offers practical strategies for businesses to thrive by embracing mindfulness.

Through 17 thought-provoking chapters, the book provides insights into the political landscape, the psychology of consumer behavior, and the importance of employee well-being and organizational health. It highlights how businesses can navigate economic challenges, foster innovation, and build a positive organizational culture. The book also emphasizes the significance of sustainability, corporate social responsibility, and ethical business practices.

By integrating mindfulness into decision-making processes, businesses can make more informed and ethical choices that benefit their bottom line, employees, customers, and the wider community. The future of the mindful marketplace is one that prioritizes sustainability, social responsibility, and technological innovation.

Ideal for business leaders, entrepreneurs, and professionals, "The Mindful Marketplace" offers a holistic approach to business that considers the interconnectedness of politics, psychology, and health. It serves as a valuable resource for anyone seeking to create a more sustainable, ethical, and human-centered business environment.

www.ingramcontent.com/pod-product-compliance
Lightning Source LLC
LaVergne TN
LVHW020459080526
838202LV00057B/6044